A NOTE TO PARENTS

When your children are ready to "step into reading," giving them the right books is as crucial as giving them the right food to eat. **Step into Reading Books** present exciting stories and information reinforced with lively, colorful illustrations that make learning to read fun, satisfying, and worthwhile. They are priced so that acquiring an entire library of them is affordable. And they are beginning readers with a difference—they're written on five levels.

Early Step into Reading Books are designed for brand-new readers, with large type and only one or two lines of very simple text per page. **Step 1 Books** feature the same easy-to-read type as the Early Step into Reading Books, but with more words per page. **Step 2 Books** are both longer and slightly more difficult, while **Step 3 Books** introduce readers to paragraphs and fully developed plot lines. **Step 4 Books** offer exciting nonfiction for the increasingly independent reader.

The grade levels assigned to the five steps—preschool through kindergarten for the Early Books, preschool through grade 1 for Step 1, grades 1 through 3 for Step 2, grades 2 through 3 for Step 3, and grades 2 through 4 for Step 4—are intended only as guides. Some children move through all five steps very rapidly; others climb the steps over a period of several years. Either way, these books will help your child "step into reading" in style!

Library of Congress Cataloging-in-Publication Data
Ross, Katharine. Twinkle, twinkle, little bug / by Katharine Ross ; illustrated by Tom Brannon.
p. cm. — (Step into reading. A step 1 book) SUMMARY: Big Bird captures a lightning bug and decides to keep it in a jar.
ISBN 0-679-87666-9 (trade) — ISBN 0-679-97666-3 (lib. bdg.)
[1. Fireflies—Fiction. 2. Birds—Fiction. 3. Puppets—Fiction.] I. Brannon, Tom, ill. II. Title. III. Series: Step into reading. Step 1 book. PZ7.R719693Tw 1996 [E]—dc20 94-48341

Printed in the United States of America 10 9 8 7 6 5 4 3 2 1

STEP INTO READING is a trademark of Random House, Inc.

Step into Reading™

Twinkle, Twinkle, Little Bug

A Step 1 Book

by Katharine Ross
illustrated by Tom Brannon

Featuring Jim Henson's Sesame Street Muppets

Random House/Children's Television Workshop

One night
Big Bird saw something
glowing in the dark.
"Look!" he said.
"A lightning bug!"

TWINKLE, TWINKLE, TWINKLE
went the lightning bug.

"Come here, little bug!
I won't hurt you,"
said Big Bird.
He put the lightning bug
in a jar.

TWINKLE, TWINKLE, TWINKLE

went the lightning bug.

"Ernie, look at my
lightning bug,"
said Big Bird.
"Twinkle for Ernie,
little bug."

TWINKLE, TWINKLE, TWINKLE

went the lightning bug.

"Zoe, look at my
lightning bug,"
said Big Bird.
"Twinkle for Zoe,
little bug."

TWINKLE, TWINKLE, TWINKLE

went the lightning bug.

"Bert, look at my
lightning bug,"
said Big Bird.
"Twinkle for Bert,
little bug."

But the lightning bug
would not twinkle.

"Why won't you twinkle,
little bug?"
asked Big Bird.

"Maybe he's lonely,"

said Bert.

Big Bird talked to
the little bug
so he would not be lonely.

But the lightning bug
would not twinkle.

17

"Maybe he's tired,"
said Elmo.

Big Bird gave
the lightning bug
a pillow
so he could
take a nap.

But the lightning bug
would not twinkle.

"Maybe he's hungry,"
said Cookie Monster.

Big Bird gave the
lightning bug one of
Cookie Monster's
cookies to eat.

But the lightning bug
would not twinkle.

"Maybe he wants
to hear some music,"
said Hoots the Owl.

Hoots played some jazz.
Big Bird joined in.
"Twinkle, twinkle,
little bug!"
sang Big Bird.

But the lightning bug
still would not twinkle.

"Grover, why won't
my lightning bug twinkle?"
asked Big Bird.
"I talked to him.
I gave him a pillow
to sleep on.
I gave him a cookie to eat.
I played music for him.
I am his friend!"

"Would <u>you</u> twinkle
if you were
stuck in a jar?"
asked Grover.
"Gee," said Big Bird,
"I guess not."